A Hundred Pairs of Eyes

A Hundred Pairs of Eyes

Poems by

Carole Croll

Cover design by Shay Culligan

ISBN: 978-1-954353-08-4

Kelsay Books
502 South 1040 East, A-119
American Fork, Utah, 84003

This book is dedicated to my family,

as we were,

as we are,

whoever we become,

always.

Acknowledgments

Over the course of my last twenty-plus years of writing poetry, there have been so many individuals and groups who have contributed both time and talent in their sincere efforts to refine and perfect my work. I gratefully acknowledge them below.

The Illinois State Poetry Society and Alan Harris, Wilda Morris, Caroline Johnson, and Barbara Eaton.

The Arbor Hill Gang

College of DuPage - Kathy Fitch, Ida Hagman, Mardelle Fortier

North Central College - David Starkey

The Bucks County Community College Poet Workshops

The Meeting House Writers

Studio B and Jane Stahl, The Rhythm and Verse Salon

Carla Eisenberg

Linda and Zak Winokur, Geri Ann Mclaughlin, Tom Mallouk

Jonathan Croll, my husband, who takes care of everything else so I can take care of poetry

I recently met a man whose kind attention and insightful commentary have fostered my growth as a poet, a person whose humor, intensity, and consideration have prompted me to clarify and project my work. With heartfelt appreciation, I acknowledge Dr. Christopher Bursk.

Contents

Acorn

A family of oaks, a deliberate planting, a park,
we stand in memory of someone loved. Maples

and pines are not among us, nor flowers, benches,
plaques. We form a grove, not woods, a tended place

for rows and rows of oak trees. We are old and wise
like forest trees, cultured in ways they are not.

We condone the ruckus of circling mowers, occasional
dogs and walkers, a road with its distractions, farmland

now entrusted. Deer do not sleep among us; we do
not feel like safety. A woman often visits. We are her

keeper. You are the next to thrive here. Be mindful
of both worlds. Persist beneath mercurial skies that

rule with light and water. Indulge the indecisive soil;
it strives to brace and nourish. Give welcome to the

darting squirrels, fling color over Autumn. Be resolute
toward human kind. *They know not what they do.*

Sky Light

Tonight I watched
the moon
through an ice encrusted
skylight
making its white journey
over black
and boundless space:
solitary orbiter,
familiar,
commonplace.

I stared
in silence, marveled
as each prism
seized the light,
designing in
the darkness
on the window's
weathered face:
an iridescent moonstone,
a crystal carapace.

Colors

Ode to My Cat—for Mingus and Billy Collins

Some day I will remember this indigo
afternoon, how you followed me to the red

chair and jumped. How the weight of you
on my denim lap felt warm and soft and

smooth. How you turned your head and those
clear green eyes looked back at me and blinked.

I had been noticing your fleecy fur, that white
rim around the tips of your ears, the hard gray

color of your tail and all the silvers in between.
I had been considering the many ways you

accompanied, saved me through the worst
of times. How you were there for me when

I lived alone, waited by the door for my return,
slept through the nights on my pillow. I recalled

you as a kitten, your fearlessness, those shaky
legs, the time you got stuck behind the stereo.

So I decided to write this poem, set it down right
now like the poem about the *oranges, the bean*

*grinder on the counter, the small coin
of that moment,* an excerpt for tomorrow.

The Notion of Brown

Yellow is passe'; orange, gauche; crimson,
so last month. Nature is Novembering.
Russet is the new red. Any tree

that's still in vogue is sporting it.
Gold is out. Bronze is in. Mahogany
is the tint of choice for leaves

intent on clinging. Field plants
accessorize in shades of brick
and ochre, fanning out

in crisper, snappier versions
of their summer selves, while
the notion of brown remains

unchanged amid Fall's fascinations.
Artfully tailored for stems, limbs,
and trunks that rise to Pleiades' skies

is brown: classic, reimagined, like the cold.

Vagabond

Fawn emerged from the tall, wind-
tossed meadow grass and stepped

with confidence onto the soft mat
of our freshly mowed front lawn.

We watched from a window as it
made its way to sidewalk,

a conspicuous path that curved
around a bordering unit of town

homes. Without apparent fear the small
and spotted youngling continued its

meandering journey through our paved
and peopled neighborhood before

stepping, ever so placidly, into
the obscurity of meadow again,

unaware that we had seen, and unaware
of the bewilderment we felt as we searched

for the wise and protective doe
who did not follow close behind.

Serenade . . . sigh

Tree frogs
are silent. Bulldozers
dredged their home,

a makeshift basin for
immoderate rainfall.
Ah, the concerts;

I reminisce. Tiny bows
on tiny strings playing
to the night. The reeds miss

them, the rushes, cat tails,
sedges, even the moon
and stars. We all miss them.

But the breeze is saddest of all,
nothing to do with its ample arms
but muffle the moans

of mourners, gather tears
that fall in the night, bury
the bones of a pond.

Stopping by Woods on a Shifty Evening

after Robert Frost

You think you know whose woods these are,
That villager, so jocular,
He would not mind your stopping by
To contemplate an evening star.

Your little horse, so keen and spry,
Has sensed that something is awry.
He stomps his hooves and shakes his bells,
He pricks his ears to testify.

These woods are home to eerie spells,
He cautions with persistent knells.
You must not idle in the sweep,
Although the downy snow compels.

The road ahead is slick and steep,
When darkness falls, mad demons creep.
Make haste for home and hearth and sleep.
Make haste for home and hearth and sleep.

Secret

Do you liken it to stone, a nugget
in the heart, something

to haul about, conceal judiciously
as it scuffs your tender conscience?

Do you think it will dissolve on its own,
wash away one day in a fit of tears?

It won't. And you are mistaken. It is not stone.
It has wings. That's what you feel, large,

swift wings chafing your frail, bone-
bound chest. Secrets want out. Ask anyone

who has one. They will tell you it is so.
What to do, what to do? Some can't take

the chafing. They blurt the truth and wail
as the winged ones peck away. Peck the eyes

that had not seen, the minds that did not know.
Peck and pierce the beating core. I differ. I spare

the doe-eyed other, allow the wings to flail
and froth, exhaust themselves within me.

With every peck I fester, my inner sanctum rots.
It is my privilege and accommodation… until

I breathe again. This cycle, this pattern, this rhythm;
it works. Look at me. Can you tell?

Missing the Boat

Like a pier I have stood a long while, witness
to vessels that cast off tethers, churn away

from shore. Like a dock I am here, anchored
to the depths that define me and my place.

I hear a horn and holler back, my bridge of words
weakening, growing faint as the boat sails on, decisive

and beautiful as a bride. I am not alone. Like me,
the harbor-bottom remains, the shore-line with its pebbles,

gulls and terns who squat and squabble, the sky
with its sun and stars forever fixed. Even the complexities

of water do not retreat from me. I can rely on both calm
and storm. Their presence dispels solitude. What happens

after makes me quake. It begins with the sighting, an un-
mistakable shape, the blast of a familiar horn, the purr

of approaching engines. Flurry on deck. Flurry up and down
the planks. Flurry in the berth. Now is the quickening.

Dusk

She sits on rocks that line a shallow pond.
Evening clouds with dimpled cheeks cast pink

across the twilight. Urgent fish tails slap and splash
in swift, unrhythmic intervals, interrupt all quietness,

recalibrate reflections. Newly crafted texture
punctuates the static scene, spindle-bodied artistry,

impressionistic renderings. Sitting as she is, alone
on a jumble of rocks, a woman become a gypsy,

a gypsy cloaked in sundown, she peers into her
crystal, the globe of emerald water, questions all

the spirits close beneath the slapping fish tails,
those that occupy the deep or float across the wrinkles.

An answer will be evident, this she knows with
certainty, certain as the Milky Way, that bale fire

in the amplitude of cold unmeasured space, a trail
beyond the withering dusk, a thoroughfare in starlight.

The Door

Your manner is a summer door, so
open I think I can walk right in,
be friends. As I step

nearer, the door moves ever
so slightly. When I reach it,
it shuts, winter tight! I peer

through the glass and see you
there, wearing your smile; you
know the one. Then come

the words that match that smile,
a succession of clever compliments
concealing a rejection. Warmth frosts

the glass, blurring the impressions you seem
to be so sure of, clouding me completely,
until—you disappear.

Aftermath

May as well be a cloud overhead,
so voluminous and plush you want
to rise up from the ragged earth

to touch me, float with me across
the sky, shape-shifting as we go.
Or I could be the line at the edge

of the perilous sea, the line that lures
you from the shore with promises
of treasure, bewitches you to follow,

retreats as you approach. Might
as well be a howl on the wind
of a savage night, the one that startles

you from sleep and keeps you awake
to wonder. Or I could be a gem
in a vault of ancient bedrock.

It's all the same to me. It's all the same
for you. Here, in the astonishing aftermath,
I am inaccessible.

Auto Biography

We were a pair, certainly not head-turning
as we drove by but attractive in our own
way, understated. There was nothing racy

or come-hither about our passing appearance,
just a stately kind of look in midnight blue,
leather, and blonde. We suited each other

in every respect. Spunky, but not too fast.
Reliable, but not in a stuffy way. Spontaneous
as a sun roof. We went everywhere together and

I cannot say I ever felt dismissed. There was no pre-
occupation with technology, no flirting in parking
lots or showing off on the highway. We took good

care of each other too. I made the appointments
and the car did the rest, navigated through the worst
of snow and rain. Relationships change over time.

They all do. Ours too. It started with a drip I tried
to fix—ended in a puddle I couldn't ignore. So we
split. It was hard, real hard, and I never saw that car

again. I'm in another arrangement now. It's respectable,
comfortable, white. I'm happy but it's not the same.
Can it be that I have loved a car?

Java

Spark the day with a shot of Java,
dark and rich from a demitasse.
Coat your throat in a flow of lava.
Nothing sparks like a shot of Java.

Boost your break with a jolt of Java,
steamy black from a hefty mug.
Add some perk to a tiresome drama.
Nothing boosts like a jolt of Java.

Soothe the day with the joy of Java,
creamy brown from a china cup.
Pair with cake or some sweet cassava.
Nothing soothes like the joy of Java.

Bread

Is any other food as sensuous
as bread?

Bread, light and airy, dainty as a damsel
in a gossamer dream. Bread, dark and grainy,
hearty and solid as a hero on a steed. Bread,

soft curves and floured crust flirting
from the baker's shelf, a fair and fickle
maiden. Bread, all seeded edge

and coarsely textured surfaces posing
like a chiseled cheek, a stubble-bearded
man. Bread, round and smooth, yielding

to a squeeze like an acquiescent breast. Bread,
dense and contoured, flexing like a muscled
chest, a Herculean man. Bread, paired with wine

and a portion of cheese splayed on the breadboard.
Mmmmmm. Bread, warm as candlelight, loaf-
full of bliss, poised for the mouth, a buttery kiss.

Eden

I selected the handblown tumbler,
(my Granny used that word).
It is small, juice-sized,

the glass thicker than most.
You feel the difference in your hand,
on your lips. They know.

With dabs of color, equator-like around,
it is beautifully blue all over.
You might imagine sea or sky.

I see a field of cornflowers, a poppy
here and there, a solitary butterfly,
marigolds and lavender.

I poured some milk, rich, the real
kind, the kind that leaves a trace,
and chose a block of chocolate

from the cache. I settled on the softest
chair for tiny tastes and measured sips, a bite
and then a swig. As dark gave way to icy

white and white deferred to dark,
temptation swirled across
my tongue.

Who said it was an apple?

Sheets

Spring has finally arrived, time to remove
the flannel sheets until the next cold season.

As I carry them to the washer, a loosely tangled
ball, I am reminded of the virus. They were

on the bed when the news erupted, soothed me
through the initial stages of lockdown, transported

my dreams, more frequent and vivid while
I waited for normal to return.

       *   *   *

It is summer now, almost fall. The sheets lie
neatly folded and stacked on the linen closet

shelf, no trace of the corona shape they once
resembled. They are smooth and uninflated.

Now I toss and turn on top of a thread count,
keep a window open. Fresh air is still okay.

       *   *   *

When winter comes I will open that closet, reach for
those sheets, envelop my bed. I wonder how the world

will be. I wonder if new normal
will sleep peacefully on flannel.

The Kite

The sun is bright, the air is clear,
the winds proclaim a holiday.
The kite you gave me months ago
is disinclined to disobey.

It leaps and climbs in maiden flight
and tugs me toward the lavish sky.
It soars above the field and trees
and makes me wish that I could fly.

It beckons to the drifting clouds,
that flock of wooly lambs,
then swoops and dives with stylish flair,
inscribing unseen monograms.

A nearby hawk flies by to note
the presence of this caller rare
that hovers in bright rainbow wings,
disrupts her game of solitaire.

I pull the string; the kite retires
and settles on a hill,
the former scribe and acrobat,
now earthbound as a daffodil.

I look above to see the sky
now solemn and alone,
a sky where clouds and hawk
and wind
and kite
and I
had flown.

Deer

All the trees were hers for she regarded
their silence in silence, learned
from them the art of being still.

The creek was hers as well. When
she dipped her tongue, it gave itself away.

The hills belonged to her. They rose
and fell with ease beneath her feet
and she never tired of climbing.

When we found her
she was gone,
a spray of hair
like ice-frosted needles
on a bed of Autumn leaves,
a row of teeth
in a partially hidden skull,
protruding bones,
nothing more.

She is ours whispered the trees, breaking
their silence, wavering, like wind.

She is mine babbled the creek, holding
tight to its waters, gliding past
the rounded rocks.

The deer belongs to me sighed the hill,
wrapping her in its leafy slope,
cradling the hollow hooves and falling,
only falling.

Learn

They are mindful of your company.
Go to the woods and be summoned.
Find a way through problematic

undergrowth and step among the trunks.
Wind here and there and back. Walk
until you feel a pull, a personal

invitation, then lower yourself to the earth's
soft saddle, lean your back against the bark,
prepare to be enlightened in the presence

of a tree. Leaves are a distraction, pawns
of the wind. They flap and twist with
color but their story is familiar,

a repetitive tale. Ignore their flutter. They will
fall to earth, curl beneath your feet and be gone.
You must listen to the timber, the seasoned shaft

in numbered rings, heart-wood of the forest,
core. Consider the trunk, how it faces north
and stiffens through the cold. Acknowledge

the bole, how it faces south and defies
the hurricane, though branches scatter
in the rush. Like you it has given all

and given in, more than some or not
as much. The forest confirms this truth.
How old is this tree? Old enough

to remember drought, old enough to record
abundance, old enough to have birthed a grove,
a hundred thousand seeds, old enough

to recognize that adaptation means survival,
compromise with rocks and soil, mostly
other trees. How wise is this tree?

Wise enough to know its family, wise enough
to heed the seasons, offer shelter, stand alone,
wise enough to trust how roots can anchor

and secure, wiser still to keep ascending
nearer, nearer to the stars.

Identify

I will tell. Moments matter,
the ones I write about, the ones
I reserve for poetry. They are
singular. They record

the world as it reveals itself
to me. They define who I am.
At times I am witness,
the only one

to see a nesting heron, red fox,
eagle atop a tree line, snake
in the water. To see what no other
eyes but mine have seen,

I must commemorate. I am sure
they speak to one another, the birds
and trees and water that populate
my pages, tell each other

tales of our meeting, how our
paths crossed unexpectedly.
Or was it planned? Did the
council of plants and animals,

the co-op of earth and sky decide
I am a worthy interpreter of tongues,
like whale, a keeper of records?
I hear the doe say,

Tell me again about the day you found
my bones on the hillside nearly hidden
in the leaves. You knew about the trees,
the creek, how they missed me.

I hear the rock say, Remember the day
you jumped? You were terrified. I edged
back so you could slip into the water
without bruising against my face. I hear

the river say, *clear to the bottom,*
shimmery on top, deliberate
and unperturbed, a suitable portrayal
most days, and I reel from the affinity.

I let you find me.
I let you see me.
I let you know me,
they say.

Witness

Marsh Creek State Park

I paddled to a point along shore where trees hung
over water, bursting with blossoms and fragrant
with honeysuckle, a shade-freckled refuge with

lapping wavelets and a glimpse of lake bottom.
A large school of minnows, perhaps a hundred,
basked in the warmth of shallows, moved as one,

entertained my underwater observations. During
this quiet moment of communion an unexpected
visitor approached, the small oval of its head

leading a succession of brown and black esses
through the clarity of edge-water. A genius
in patterning and an artist in locomotion,

the snake posed no threat to me. It skimmed
through the ripples with intention, a purpose
unique to itself. Without a glance it passed

the orange of my kayak, proceeding on its
mission until its head, a mere dot on broad
expanse of lake, disappeared. I am reminded

that of all the inhabitants of Earth,
it was this snake, this particular snake
who passed me by that day,

and it was I and only I who noticed, unless
you include the minnows, motionless as statues,
fearfully suspended, a hundred pairs of eyes.

Hay

I came across a field at dusk.
Freshly mown, it was, with stalks

that lay in sprawling mounds
upon the stubble, a pale green
sea, still on the surface, tumbled

like the tide, shallow and inviting.
I did not wade. I stood like a child

at the edge of the surf, hay-smell
warm as a sunny day, cool as a milky
moon, clean as a rain-rinsed thunder sky,

dry as the withered wind, sweet
as the buffalo grass of summer,

sad, for it was done. And
the scent rose wild and high
as a hill, engulfing me

the way salt spray does,
the way sea foam does,

the way scrubbed sand does
at the shoreline.
Rose like a wave from

the sea, it did,
and carried me away.

Ten Point

You gave morning unexpected brilliance,
standing beside the tangled brush as you did,

your brow bearing the weight of its massive crown,
eyes not shifting. Majesty with a brown flank.

What was it about me, a two-legged crossing
the open field between us, silent, observing,

stilled by the sight of you? What was it
that impelled your leaving, your amble

into the complicated branches, your escape
from my gaze?

There was no urgency in your step. No raised
white tail, no snap from startled twigs, no

troubled leap across the brook and race into
the woods. I had seen doe a dozen times…

Only moments passed before I saw
your face again,

realized you had reconsidered
our encounter, my presence,

custardy-white in a jacket and hood,
slow-footed and head-bowed in the wind.

Sea Glass

Birthed by the sea,
plucked from the sand
on a morning walk, I want
to be a gem in the palm
of Neruda. Safe on the raft
of his hand, I want him
to look at me, lift me
to the light, see me
the way he saw *topaz,*
like the sun's anatomy,
congealed honey, sky
salt. What would he say?
Welcome to the blue
of Sapphire Tower, desert
petals born of wind
and fever. Greetings
daughter of heaven,
hue of moon-scythed
twilight time. Like marlin,
like sea star, like
bioluminescent sparkle,
children of the Pacific
Mother. *I invite you to*
sea glass, crystalline shard
on rocky shore, wave
frosted, glacial, blue
as the eye of a cyclone.

Italics: from *Stones of the Sky* by Pablo Neruda—poem *X.*
Translated by James Nolan

Coward Rock

Once.
Just once
I did it.
I braved a jump
into the cool blue.
It was a summer day
and the lake lapped gingerly
against the towering presence
of an imposing rock face, whose fame
I timidly challenged with one frail leap.

Others waited in the water below.
They hadn't struggled the way I had,
hadn't harbored apprehensions.
They'd leaped with sheer abandon—
and then the time was mine.
My turn to conquer,
slay the dragon,
take the plunge,
let go.
Fly!

Photograph

We stepped outside on the little
porch at the front of the house
to view rainclouds in the east,

then looked west to where
the sun hung low above a tree
line at the far end of the prairie.

Despite the sun the rain came
down, filled the space beneath
the clouds like a curtain of beads,

tangled itself in the tufted tops
and deep among the stalks
of slender grass. We could have

gathered liquid gems, crowned our
heads with diadems, but looked to the east
where colors merged from warm to cool

to icy cold. Snapped a picture of the sky,
and though we pleaded and beguiled,
the downturned rainbow never smiled.

Tides

I rode a blue wave when tide was high, flat
on my back like a scrap of wood. It lifted me

to the Atlantic sky where I dreamed that I could
surely fly until it set me down. I lingered at its

balmy base until another took its place. To the azure
sky and back I fell, my dream adrift, a broken spell.

I sensed a change in the fickle tide, watched as
the waters large and wide receded into steely deep,

wondered what the ocean would not keep or hide
away, what secret it might reveal that day. I walked

the beach when tide was low. As the sun boiled in the sky
I feared that I might liquefy or bake into a crust of salt.

It was then I spied a perfect shell, as yet untouched by human
hands or harmed in the salty under-lands beneath the wavy

sea, the one that had been so good to me when I was a scrap
of wood, you see, dreaming I could surely fly. A perfect shell

on the steamy sand, pink as the east at break of dawn, patterned
around like the back of a fawn, spiraling endlessly into itself,

a point on its top like the hat of an elf. This, the ocean
gave to me, and an almost ride to the sky for free.

And Beautiful Tuesday Said

This day is for you, breathe
deep. Draw long and slow
and full. I have swaddled
the hours in lucent warmth,
coddled them to stay.
Be mindful of these moments.
Tomorrow comes the chill.

The sky is a field of sapphires
with a single golden bloom.
It glazes the day
with its petals, look up,
look all around.

I've flattered the trees and now
they blush in whispered shades
of red. Others I've brushed
with yellow dawn,
excepting those who favor
green and stand like
bridesmaids, patient for
the morrow.

The sound of this confection,
a crinkle in the breeze, the scent
is crisp, like brittle sticks
that snap beneath your feet.

This Autumn day is made
for you, partake 'til you are full.
I may not serve a slice like
this in quite this way again.

Birds!

First thing I saw was the northern
sky and a pair of buzzards etching
slow, wide circles. High above

the meadow, uncommonly large,
they stood out against the gray cloud
tones of an impending storm. A flock

of smaller birds occupied the same bone-
gray sky, a formation in black that moved
as one, listed left, dropped behind a house.

I did not expect to see the flock again, turned
my attention to the sky, hillocks of mist
that rose and fell in shifts above the buzzards.

To my surprise the flock arose, a horde above
the roof. Its pattern of points, a spray of darts,
pierced the bank of a passing cloud. Whoosh!

There I stood, splotched in a sizable hollow
carved by conniving buzzards circling
high in the northern sky.

Butterfly Effect

Nothing more than egg
and promise clinging to
a leaf.

Nothing faster than a crawl
when wings are just
a dream. Nothing

but a dangle in the long
and lonely darkness.
Can you be like butterfly

if butterfly is this?
Can you live life flickering,
marking precious time

splendoring the air
that gives you prominence
and flight? Settling ever softly

on a lush and lissome
petal, can you savor
nectar in the tiniest

of portions? Can you dip
and rise as if the waltz could
last forever? Anything can happen

in the fraction of a . . .

Consolation

When I am left to wonder if the world
will come undone, I stray beneath a veil
of leaves; there the earth is well. Red tipped

shoots and white blossomed limbs prevail,
climb through a tangle of briars and rot, surge
overhead, legions and more. Gray squirrel

is alone. It races through a maze of side-swept
branches and high-rise trunks, knows all the ways
up, every way out. Brook is clear, mellow.

Relieved of rains that made it roil, it passes
unimpelled, burbles contentedness to greenery
and meadow flowers that seat along its banks.

My steps move low and slow through fields
of unmarked pathways fox and deer are known
to tread. Low and slow against the sky, sun

sheds its final ray. Dove coos lustily, ribbons
of gray hope on the down-slant of afternoon.
At times, this is enough.

Quilt

It is a curious thing to see,
a shaft of gauzy yellow,
a fox hunt, meticulously

oval and preposterous
in its presence on a bed quilt.
Juxtaposed in such a way

against the stark
triangularities
of a hand-stitched

coverlet, one might
wonder about the intention
of the seamstress. The fox,

of course, does not
wonder; it knows, understands
the language of hoof beats,

the significance of red, how
death arrives in a misstep
to the music of yelping

dogs. Catch the light, little fox.
Beam up! Leave the triangles
to the horses.

By the Sweat of its Vowels

(and Consonants)

The word "labor" toils from the page like a
seasoned hireling.

There's "l" leading off, lusty, laudable, and
"b", the other staff, backbone of the crew.

There's the somewhat round "a", all in, or
almost all in, and the obviously outstanding
"o". Oh!

And if "a" is abashed at following
such a luminous beginning,
"o" establishes its identity as open-

handed and obliging, suggesting
the kind of word that doesn't give up,
ongoing, so to speak.

That's what "o" is all about.

Along comes bossy "r". Remember elementary
school, bossy "r" and its tendency to take
over the humble vowel preceding it?

Good old bossy "r", rrrrrrrrrrrrr-ing like a pirate,
rasping to the end.

Well, time to move along, get busy.
Who me? Yes, you!

That's "labor" for you.

Lichens

I'm lichen the way you sometimes
swarm across a rock, or log, or tree
like etchings in cuneiform
or colorful calligraphy

But moss-ly

I'm lichen the way you crust and
spread across a dull and faded plain
like butter on a slab of bread
or sunlight on a stalk of grain

But moss-ly

I'm lichen the way your hearty lobes
withstand the elements at large
and propagate the pliant globe
with spores and fragments as you sparge

But moss-ly

I'm lichen the way you share your prize
of weaver's dye and medicine
and how you will not compromise
when nature's breath is wearing thin

But moss-ly

I'm lichen the way you shrub and branch
then grow up small or hang down low
a bi-organic avalanche - a thalli oratorio
Bravo!

All in the Family

"The Solar System's come undone,"
announced the Sun to everyone.

"Including me?"
wailed Mercury.

"You're such a whiny little mass,"
hissed Venus with her toxic gas.

"We've been together since my birth,"
protested patient Mother Earth.
"What can you mean, dear Father Sun?
How can the system come undone?"

"There's one of us who can't belong.
 For all these years the count's been wrong."

"Well bless the ever-blazing stars!"
roared crater-dimpled, red-cheeked Mars.

"I must concur," sighed Jupiter.
"I've looked about with my red eye;
there's one we've got to nullify."

"I can't be bothered with these things,"
sniffed Saturn as he fluffed his rings.

Uranus whirled a tilted while, then
cracked a crooked ice-blue smile.

"I think I have somewhat to say,"
huffed Neptune in a haughty way.
"I'd like to keep my orbit free
of orb-trails from that refugee."

Such talk so dimmed the Sun at noon
he hid his face behind the Moon.

"Now dears," begged Mother Earth of blue,
"There's room in space for all of you."

Then Pluto shone his distant grin
and spun his dark eccentric spin.
"Though scientists demote my worth,
I'm glad to abdicate my berth.

For though they call me dwarf and small,
I am the most renowned of all.
There's nothing to your planet show,
without my stellar cameo."

Fish Dreams

A boat plies the surface, below
the depths are full, teeming

with translucent tails. Sashaying
over mud bottoms,

skirting boulders and logs, roving
through cool thickets; I want

to catch one. I bait a hook a time
or two on many a lazy Sunday,

feel the start of a stiffened line,
frantic rush beneath me.

Reel a writhing bullet in,
drop it at my feet, close

enough to end a life, serve
it on a platter. Feed it

to the flux instead, let it slip
away. Accede to its unspoken

plea, grasping gills, vacant eyes,
a prayer in shimmering scales.

Ribbon Trail

What will
remain
when I am
gone? A
ribbon
in
the wind?
A streamer
that will
zip and
snap
and swirl
from the
wand of
time? Will
anyone
notice my
ribbon trail
when I
leave it
far behind?
Will they
ever think
to reach up
high, snatch
it from the
breeze, tie
it tight
around
a finger and
remember
me?

Threes

Sleep comes easy at three PM, that's right,
midday. A cloudy sky and patting of rain,

anthems of the wind, a blanket and book
when snow piles deep, they all play

their parts. And yet, the song of the sun
can lull as well, shadows that sprawl

on grass, the blue of the sky
that hushes eyes when a hammock

sways in June. Sleep comes hard
at three AM when all should be slack

in the night, breath in its bosom, the tongue
in its mouth, bones in their sack of flesh.

What opens eyes at a time like this
to the clock on the shelf with its green-glow

three and the shape of the chair near the wall?
What hearkens ears like a sentinel to the creaks

of an unwalked floor, the hoot from an owl
on a beam of the moon, the sound of nothing

at all?

The Lines Between

In March blue heron returns and
stands in the shallow tidewaters.

Sunlight pours through the breach
of a cloud, pale and thick and yellow,

cleansing the sky scape of clarity,
garbling exactness.

Blurred is the line between
sky and cloud, cloud

and sea, sea
and shore.

Fine is the line between
shore and bird, bird

and me, me
and sky.

So Goes the Day

Simplicity fills hollows
and makes the day round,
the way coffee and sweet

brown rolls fill out a morning
pressed thin by the weight
of the daily news, the way

solar chimes and light beams
fill in the margins of duty, break
the ennui of afternoon with a recital

by the sun. For a day is meant
to be filled out, filled in,
filled up and over,

so when the moon begins its story
and you listen until you sleep,
it will matter

that you took a walk
by a pasture after dinner,
because a cow approached the fence

and it filled up a hollow to pet her,
filled it all the way up and over,
for a day now round, complete.

Odyssey

When I am old I will remember
how the sun boiled, the river
coursed, cliffs rose tight against
current. How mud oozed, a canyon

squeezed, paths winded through sage.
I'll hear music prance on a patio, bounce
in a van over outcrops, melt in the spray
of a sun warmed shower deep inside

the woods. I'll see a ring of fire-lit faces,
pines against a stippled sky, mule deer
I could almost touch, features flanked
in moonlight. When I am old I won't

forget the mountain and its curse of thirst,
how it lashed my sluggish body, breath
too thin to breathe. I'll sit myself in a fold-
ing chair atilt on river rocks, let water-

tripping conversation spend my afternoon,
and right before the memory fades, I'll take
a plunge in the Lochsa, cool and sheer
and opulent, silk on seasoned skin.

Dream Light

If the flames subside the keeper
of the fire rises from a rumpled bed,

crosses the earth on shuffling feet, chooses
from the dwindling stack an ordinary log,

feeds it to the embers. Quick to take advantage,
air spreads its shivery wings, flaps its fanned-out

feathers in a penetrating chill, weaves its way
precisely through the fire keeper's blanket

and a mound of glowing coals that pulses
in orange and blue. Fussing and fuming

in an effort to sustain this urging of wind
and prompting of wood, coaxing of wind

and yielding of wood, pleasure of wind
and magic of wood, a flame is born where

there was none and light dispels the darkness.
Warmth supplants the feathering cold, pervades

the tattered blanket. Night succumbs to
dream light. Some fires must never die.

The Brink

When I awake I must be brave.
Though day dawns clear, a flash
at the brink of blindness, night
still wraps its tendrils round my

mind—morning time disquietude.
The sun persists, infuses haze
with light, more light, sheer light
that separates dim from keen until

the blunt dread of dayspring is dispersed.
Some is chewed and swallowed like
the contents of a fruit bowl. Some spills
down the drain in a frothy rinse. Some

is shed beside the walking path;
a scattering here a smattering there
until there is no dread, no edge, just
round, audacious, bright-eyed afternoon.

Something

Something about that field,
the way it looked at dusk,

a meadowland of daisies beside a
stretch of roadway. Young boys

jumping from a wooden bridge
into a Canadian stream, our

camp van lurching madly
as it hauled our bags of laundry.

Something about the twilight,
the chroma of the sky, the broadness

of an open field, how innocent
the daisies, night held in abeyance—

reminded me of you.

Caryatids

dedicated to Glenna Holloway, Margarete "Maggie" Cantrall, Nancy Jean Carrigan

—poets of ISPS

You bring to mind the ones we see whose
beauty braced antiquity with classic strength
and symmetry, the ones remaining
sure and tall despite

demise of roof and wall. With resolute
and patient grace they stand securely
in the place established for them
long ago. You bring to mind

the ones that still adorn where temples
long have passed, whose noble presence
holds us fast to what is grand, sublime,
and true, the ones that linger

to inspire and fuel imagination's fire,
their craftsmanship still deft and fine,
exquisite, and of rare design, without
a parallel. You bring to mind

the ones that rise, cavorting with the very
skies that swirl above them bold and blue,
the ones that dignify a stance by weathering
the tests

of time in humble intrepidity. Relieved now
of their former task and free to court
the winds at last, these pillars punctuate our
view—we, a grateful retinue.

Prayer

May I have this day
to make a poem.

Glean it from the gullet of a bird.
Water it with cool imagination.

Cultivate new landscapes
with the mention of a word.

May I have this day
to tend a poem.

Hamper any weeds that strive
to confiscate the light.

Gather from the blossoms
spoons of nectar.

Shutter petals snug against the night.
May I have this day to pluck a poem.

Feel how firm, how ripe,
how round the girth.

Sample it; indulge in the delight
of its confection.

Thank cool water, light,
a bird, the earth.

About the Author

Nothing is more satisfying than the crafting of poetry, the translation of experience into the specificity of language. Carole Croll has been crafting poetry for over twenty years. This former teacher of English language learners brings to her work a simplicity that is intelligible, refreshing. A former massage therapist, Carole recognizes the therapeutic value of touch and provides through her poetic renderings a vehicle for embracing the natural world, for palpating its beauty as it reveals itself, judiciously, candidly, and exquisitely—to her. She has been awarded by the Illinois State Poetry Society, The Nevada Poetry Society, and Poets and Patrons of Chicago. Her work has appeared in numerous publications and collections. She is the author of a volume of poetry entitled *The Gift Forthcoming,* poems of love, beauty, and spirit.

About the Artist

Bradley Wilson received a BFA in painting from the University of Tennessee at Chattanooga and an MFA from the University of Mississippi. His paintings, drawings, and sculptures are in many private and corporate collections across the United States and Canada. Wilson teaches studio art and art history at Lee University in Cleveland, Tennessee, and conducts regular painting workshops at the John C. Campbell Folk School in Brasstown, North Carolina.

Visit him at
bradleywilsonpaintings.com
or
facebook.com/bradleywilsonart

www.ingramcontent.com/pod-product-compliance
Lightning Source LLC
Chambersburg PA
CBHW031152090426
42738CB00008B/1295